NELLIE'S HILL

JILL DOUGLAS HOPPER

Author of
LAST CHANCE ALASKA

Copyright © 2014 Registration number: TXu 1-908-o712
by Jill Douglas Hopper

All rights reserved. No part of this book may be used or reproduced in any manner whatsoever without written permission of the publisher

ISBN: 14664766
Library of Congress Control Number: 34430767
Published by Hopper Publishing
Randolph, VT
Edited by Jennifer Marx
Bethel, VT

Cover Arranged by Jennifer Crowe
Pip Printing, Palm Bay, FL.

Cover photo:
Nellie in New York State. circa early 1920's
……………………Photographer unknown
Title page photo:
Nellie during a NEW YORK STATE WINTER. circa early 1920's
……………………Photographer unknown

Back cover :
OLD CLARK MILLS TEXTILE FACTORY
New York State 2000…………Photographed by Author

To order additional copies of *Nellie's Hill* or *Last Chance Alaska* contact:

https://www.createspace.com/3713883
https://www.createspace.com/900000446
Books also available in E-book at Amazon
https://www.amazon.com

https://www.lastchancealaska.com

1914

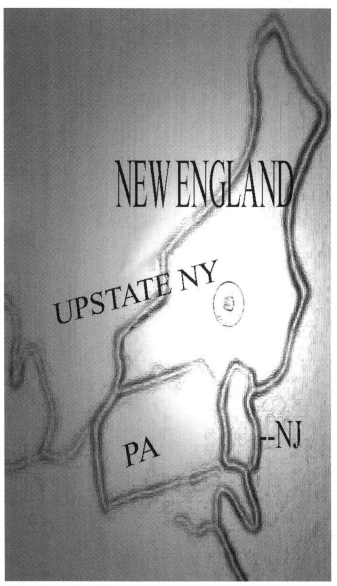

Illustration 1. Map of Upstate New York. 1914

Photo by U.E.H.

JILL DOUGLAS HOPPER
Author of *LAST CHANCE ALASKA*
Capulin Volcano National Monument, N.M. 2000

PREFACE

Motivation for writing *NELLIE'S HILL* began with a collection of forty-four letters. *"Letters into the future,"* as Nellie put it — events she could clearly remember while living with us from 1997 to 2001.

The book opens in the forested hills of the New York State interior in the very early years of the 1900's. Nellie Elizabeth was just a child. Her letters cover nearly a century of fast moving moments of this country's firsts. In uncovering the layers of those early years, some untold intriguing historical surprises emerged. The last four chapters, on the other hand, focus on Nellie as an older woman. She had lived nearly a century in this country's whirlwind of advancement.

In 2000 a cross-country road trip was planned to gather some repeat photography of photos taken by her late husband (my Dad) on his way to Alaska in 1935 prior to their meeting. She was delighted to go along.

Numerous camping trips were scheduled with Nellie to acclimate her to the world of camping, before undertaking this adventure for *LAST CHANCE ALASKA*.

CONTENTS

PREFACE by Author..v
THE LAST BEACH HOUSE by Heather Van Arsdel......56
REMARKS by Alison M. Van Arsdel........................64

CHAPTER I   A Newly Formed Family......................1
CHAPTER II   Randolph Meets Nellie 35
CHAPTER III   Life's Directions................................45
CHAPTER IV   Preparing for a Road Trip..................59
CHAPTER V   Nellie's Crossing..............................67
CHAPTER VI   Eastward Ho....................................99
CHAPTER VII   A Precious Few.............................107

Illustration 1. Map of Upstate New York 1914...............iv
Illustration 2. Moon Hill 15
Illustration 3. Three Waves of the 1918 Pandemic..........17
Illustration 4. One Room Schoolhouse........................19
Illustration 5. Styrofoam Art....................................63
Illustration 6. Road Trip Map E to W 64
Illustration 7. Road Trip Map W to E 64

A COLLECTION of Forty-four letters by Nellie C. Douglas beginning with the introduction of life's players on the hill.

LETTER 1.   My Father..3
LETTER 2.   My Mother..5
LETTER 3   My Sister Alice..6
LETTER 4.   Aunt Nellie...7
LETTER 5.   Church on the Hill....................................8
LETTER 6.   Aunt Catherine..9
LETTER 7.   Summers at the Stone House....................10
LETTER 8.   Life's Directions....................................10
LETTER 9.   Grandma Mary and Grandpa Elmer...........11
LETTER 10.   Grandma and Grandpa Morey..................12
LETTER 11.   Remembering the 1918 Influenza..............14
LETTER 12.   Our One Room Schoolhouse....................18

NELLIE'S TALES

LETTER 13.   The Mailman's Daughter.......................20
LETTER 14.   The Hindenburg..................................20
LETTER 15.   Toilets..21

CONTENTS cont'd

LETTER 16 Skiing, Sledding & Baseball...................21
LETTER 17 Stone House Tales..............................22
LETTER 18 A Country Horning............................23

FAVORITE PET NAMES circa early1900's

LETTER 19 Favorite Names for Horses....................24
LETTER 20 Favorite Names for Dogs.......................25
LETTER 21 Favorite Names for Cats.......................26
LETTER 22 Favorite Names for Cats cont'd...............27

EARLY HOLIDAYS REMEMBERED

LETTER 23 Thanksgiving.....................................28
LETTER 24 Early Christmases..........................28,29
LETTER 25 Past New Year's Eves..........................29
LETTER 26 Valentine's Day................................29
LETTER 27 Easter Memories...........................29,30
LETTER 28 July 4th Fireworks............................30
LETTER 29 Halloween Pranks..............................30

A CENTURY of FIRSTS

LETTER 30 Electricity Comes to the Hill..................31
LETTER 31 First Telephone Experiences..................31
LETTER 32 First Radio Encounter.........................31
LETTER 33 Our First Model-T.............................32
LETTER 34 First Dentist..................................32
LETTER 35 First Plane Ride..............................32

A FIFTIES KIND of FAMILY

LETTER 36 Our Wedding.................................36,37
LETTER 37 Our First Black and White TV................39
LETTER 38 About Childbirth 48
LETTER 39 Pot of Gold....................................48
LETTER 40 Baby's First Ride.............................48
LETTER 41 About Space Travel..........................52

THE WORLD ACCORDING to NELLIE

LETTER 42 Regarding Illegal Drug Use...................102
LETTER 43 Regarding Tobacco...........................102
LETTER 44 Era of Prohibition............................102

Photographer unknown

"My Aunt Catherine, with me and my brother, Bernie. We were seven and nine years of age." N.C.D.

CHAPTER I
A NEWLY FORMED FAMILY
A WELSH AMERICAN PUBLISHING?
A YOUNG MOTHER OF FOUR SUCUMBS TO COMPLICATIONS FROM TUBERCULOCIS

"My mother, Ethel Elizabeth was born June 21, 1886. She passed away on April 14, 1919. She was thirty-two years old," stated Nellie from a rocking chair in Florida in 1998. I am the author and granddaughter of Ethel Elizabeth. Those that were living during this occurrence had some difficult, troublesome decisions to make. These decisions are not for us to judge, as life moved on "ever testing" in the years that followed — back in the second decade of the early nineteen hundreds.

Was it raining on that narrow dirt road leading to the Evergreen Cemetery deep in the hills of upper New York State? Was it chilly? Could we hear the mourners openly expressing grief? As horse and carriages prepared to leave, where were the three children? How did a family of six fade to a family of four in a matter of a few short years?

The photograph on the opposite page appears to be the only one taken of the "newly formed family." It was taken in the back yard of Nellie's Aunt and Uncle's home in Upstate New York. Nellie and her youngest brother, unexpectedly had a new surrogate Mom and Dad. Nellie's oldest brother was relocated to a nearby town in the valley to live with his father, who worked as a trolley car driver.

Growing up, we had heard many stories about "the hill." Nellie referenced it many times how hard it was walking to her many school activities in the valley. A hill that seemed to grow steeper as the years went on. I often wondered what it would have been like hiking up that hill with sleet blowing in my face? In the very early years of Nellie's childhood there was a one room schoolhouse further up the hill from her Aunt and Uncle's home. Her high school was down in the valley. This strenuous exercise Nellie endured as a child undoubtedly led to her longevity.

From the "Newly Formed Family" photo on page viii and a life that was lived to its fullest, Nellie Elizabeth graduated from the Eastman School of Music in Rochester, New York, married in 1940, raised three children and ran a music school in northern New Jersey until surrendering to old age. The chapters in *Nellie's Hill* are designed to provoke thought.

Photographer unknown

"My Mom and Dad." circa 1905 N.C.D

LETTER 1 MY FATHER 1886—1965

At Mom's funeral, my Dad cried bitterly as he laid over the casket. Mrs. Bates took the three of us back to her home while they went to the cemetery to bury our mother. My oldest brother, Chester broke down and sobbed. Bernie and I seeing Chester cry so hard, joined him.

My dad, Homer Jay died March 10, 1965. He was lots of fun with a good sense of humor. He was average height with warm brown eyes.

Dad never remarried after my mother's death. Many years he was a trolley car motorman in the valley of a New York State town. He liked music and he enjoyed strumming the banjo. One of his favorite songs was, "Yes, I Have No Bananas," but he sang and liked many songs.

Dad visited my youngest brother and me at Aunt Catherine and Uncle Roswell's house frequently. I will always remember his suspenders. He and Chester boarded at Mrs. Bates' home, which was right behind a theatre on Miller Street in the valley. The theatre was called the Miller Street Theatre.

Later, Dad bought a little farm in the hills of New York State, where he resided until entering a nursing home. He had a heart problem from which he died at age seventy-eight. Dad was always lively and full of exuberance!!! Homer Jay was a much loved man. He was good to everyone! I was always <u>proud to say he was my father!</u>

N.C.D.

Photographer unknown
A family in mourning and a picture speaking out, circa 1919

Photographer unknown
"My mother, Ethel Elizabeth" N.C.D. circa 1905

LETTER 2   MY MOTHER 1886—1919

My mother was Ethel Elizabeth. She was in the Oneida County Tubercular Hospital for four years until her death in 1919. She had contracted pneumonia there and died of complications.

Before marriage, Mom worked in the *Clark Mills Textile Factory. People said you could always tell what color wool they were working on by the color of the water in the Oriskany Creek.

I was born at home in the valley in 1912. I was about two years old when Mom was placed into the Oneida Tubercular Hospital. She used to call me, "My baby." I had three older siblings. My sister Alice was the oldest with my brothers Chet and Bernie following.

It was thought that my sister Alice contracted Tuberculosis from my mother while nursing her as a baby. The Dr. advised my mother not to nurse her babies anymore because of the risk of contracting TB. Mom then used a towel to protect us from the TB. Aunt Catherine would invite my mother to visit us on the hill several times a year.

I remember coming home from school one day and Aunt Catherine asked me to go into the house and bring her out a pan from behind the door of the pantry. Mother was hiding behind that door. I was so surprised and excited to find her there. We hugged each other. I was about seven years old at that time.

Aunt Catherine would provide my mother with a brown paper bag into which my mother would spit phlegm. Aunt Catherine would also tear up little pieces of paper for her to use and then she would take the pieces outdoors and burn them.

I remember my mother would bring us small gifts when she would come to visit us. I recall Mother bringing me a handmade handkerchief with tatting around the edges.

I also remember Mom sending a number of post cards to Bernie and myself at my Aunt's house. She frequently opened her post cards with "My dear children." Mother's skin was fair and her eyes were blue. Her hair was auburn like my daughter Jill's.   N.C.D.

*The Clark Mills Textile Factory was named after the Clark brothers, who opened a textile mill on the Oriskany Creek in 1846 — located in a Hamlet in Clark Mills, New York. The mills operated until the mid-20th century.

LETTER 3   *MY SISTER ALICE 1905 — 1915*

My sister was born on September 18. Alice was at least seven years older than I was. She died of Tuberculosis.

Doctors in removing Alice's tonsils accidentally clipped off the end of her voice box, which impeded her speech. At night, often times, she would cry herself to sleep. Dad had his bed along side Alice's bed and would hold her hand until she dropped off to sleep.

Photographer unknown
"Alice M. was my only sister" N.C.D. circa 1908-10

Alice Mabel could talk, but her speech was not clear. Mother was frequently in the hospital with illness during this time. Alice died four years before Mom did. Dad was devastated at Alice's death. Aunt Catherine, who later raised me, told me that my Dad was overwhelmed when Alice died and said she never saw anyone sob so hard as Dad did at Alice's funeral. Alice is buried at a cemetery in or near the upstate town I grew up in. This photo of Alice always hung in the downstairs sitting area of Dad's country home.

In the early years many people had their children's tonsils removed so they wouldn't cough so much. Alice, Chet, Bernie and I all had our tonsils removed.

Alice was named after my Aunt Alice (Aunt Catherine's sister) who died when she was twenty-one, giving birth to her only son, Roy.   N.C.D.

A watermark photo on page iii reflects a family beginning to fall apart. Their sister Alice would die in a year and their mother Ethel Elizabeth would be gone in five. Why Alice was not included in this photo is unclear. The only photo of her is the one to the left on page 6. She was very, very sick.

1914

LETTER 4   *AUNT NELLIE*

As I remember my Aunt Nellie, she reminded me very much of my mother. She had the same color hair and good nature. Her eyes were blue and she was slender of build. Aunt Nellie was about five feet tall. I was her name sake. Unfortunately, I never had a photo of her.

Aunt Nellie rode the same bus to her work that I rode going to high school. For a while I didn't recognize her, but when I did , I spoke to her. This took place around my second year in high school. Aunt Nellie always spoke to me until I graduated from high school. I didn't see her anymore after that, until her death. Aunt Catherine did not encourage a relationship with her and remarked, *"Your mother would have lived a lot longer if she didn't have a sister."* Aunt Catherine was fearful of loosing my brother and me, noted Nellie Elizabeth looking back.

I was home from college when Aunt Nellie died. I remember she had a heart condition. We all attended her funeral in the valley. Aunt Nellie's son Charles came, too. Aunt Catherine invited Charles to her home after the service, but was less than cordial to him. Charles stopped over to family members in the valley after visiting up on the hill. My oldest brother was among them.

Charles moved to eastern Pennsylvania to one of the big cities there and that was the last I heard from him — the name "Anna" was scratched on a piece of paper above the funeral paragraph. *"She may have been a wife, or daughter to Charles,"* noted the author.   N.C.D.

LETTER 5   *MY CHURCH DAYS*

I went to Sunday school and church when I was young. The church was located on Frankfort Hill. It was a good mile or two above the school house on the left. There wasn't a cemetery there. It was also a white wooden structure like the school. I am sure that the church is no longer there. The four of us attended together — My Aunt and Uncle, my brother and myself. My oldest brother attended his own church regularly in the valley.

The church I attended was Protestant. My mother never got to attend church with me. She attended church where she lived. We all were baptized.   N.C.D

WALLS by Author

Nellie's birth in the early 1900's was seldom, if ever, discussed while we were growing up. It was like it did not exist. Also, the mention of grandparents from Nellie's mother's side was non existent and we were not made aware of their names. Years later accompanied by Nellie, my husband, Emory and I visited the cemetery where Nellie's parents and and Aunt Nellie were buried, placing together some of the missing pieces to her life. This visit is discussed on Page 49 of chapter III.

Only until recently did I realize why the concealment was kept. Several years ago, we acquired a white and tan spotted dog from a campground in South Carolina, while heading home to Florida from our usual east coast summer camping treks. We named the dog Jake and he became an immediate *"loved"* member of our family. Jake came from dubious means. He had heart worms and a bad skin condition. The campground owners said he had arrived at their doorstep with an appalling rope burn around his neck as he attempted to free himself. Jake finally chewed his way out of his dilemma and we eventually adopted him.

We never returned to that campground and to this day, we drive straight through without stopping. Jake now leads *"our"* pack and we must protect him, as he protects us.

The aunt who raised Nellie and the younger of her two brothers lived in constant fear of loosing them. Nellie's mother had a sister named Nellie, who was living in the United States. She would have been a logical candidate to raise Nellie (her namesake) and her brother. Walls were put up. *"Your mother would have lived a lot longer if she..."*

Photographer unknown
"Catherine Irene was the Aunt that raised me." N.C.D. circa early 1900's

LETTER 6 *AUNT CATHERINE (nicknamed, Kate)*

   March was my birth month. Aunt Catherine would always bake a cake for this occasion. I remember my birthday as a happy time. My brother and I were especially cheerful when our older brother happened to be visiting.

   One birthday, Mother gave me a hand crocheted light pink outfit for my doll and I had to pretend to like it. She was present when I received it and I didn't want to hurt her feelings. I did not really care that much for dolls when I was young. My Dad asked me one year what I wanted for my birthday and I told him a pink knitted top, which he gave me. I was about seven or eight years old. I liked it very much.

                                                N.C.D.

LETTER 7   *SUMMERS at the STONE HOUSE*

Grandma Mary had blue eyes and was of slender build and medium height. Her hair was light brown. When my mother died Grandma and Grandpa were already along in age and had raised ten children of their own, so my father asked Aunt Catherine to raise my youngest brother and me. Each summer Aunt Catherine and Uncle Roswell would take us to the Stone House to spend two weeks with our grandparents. Aunt Catherine would usually stay with us. In the beginning we traveled by horse and carriage. The trip took all day to go through those interior New York State woods on narrow, dusty dirt roads. Later we went by Model-T.

Another Aunt would come each summer from St. Louis with her children and spend two weeks at the Stone House with Grandpa and Grandma. My oldest brother came to North Bay by train and Grandpa would pick him up by horse and wagon at the train depot. Aunt Ruth would stay and help her parents with the grandchildren.   N.C.D.

LETTER 8   *LIFE'S DIRECTIONS*

My Grandpa Elmer taught us many things. He always said, *"know where your feet are pointing before you take off running."*

Refer page viii

Grandpa Elmer Jay had long whiskers. He was very slender with brown eyes and hair — average height. He lived to his early eighties and died of "old age" at Aunt Catherine's home. Many times I said, "Tell us again Grandpa about you and your Dad going off to the Civil War." Grandpa was only fifteen years old when he headed for the Civil War in November of 1862. His father, Pardon T. wouldn't allow him to go alone, so he grabbed his hat and went with him. Grandpa bought a shirt for his friend because of the bugs. He would march for us and we grandchildren would sit in front of the Stone House and watch and clap.

N.C.D.

Photographer unknown

"Grandma Mary and Grandpa Elmer." N.C.D. circa early 1900's

LETTER 9 MY GRANDMA and GRANDPA

Grandma and Grandpa raised ten children at the Stone House. There were four boys and six girls. Their home was built by Grandpa out of stone from his nearby woods. It was located deep in the New York Sate interior.

The two youngest died early. One died when he was only a toddler. He was hit in the head with a stone thrown by a boy walking by. They were out in front of the house. He was two or three years old. Grandpa began making him a little white dress. He died about a week later. He had developed a temperature. He was the youngest boy.   N.C.D.

Note: Back in 1913, at age sixty-six, Elmer Jay Clarke attended the fifty year government sponsored reunion of the end of the Civil War. Recently, a one hundred year commemorative exhibit of the North South convention was displayed at the visitor center museum in Gettysburg, PA. Elmer's hat, mess plate, spoon, identification tag and photos were donated by Marty N. Wilson and the Norton family.

LETTER 10 *GRANDPA and GRANDMA MOREY*

Grandma Morey was my first piano teacher. They asked if we would mind having our children call them "*Grandpa* and *Grandma*," because they had no children of their own. I was flattered and agreed. I studied piano with her when I was in grade school and with Mary Nightingale when I was in high school.

Grandma Morey was slight of build and had bright blue eyes and fair skin. She and her husband Ezra (photograph unavailable) had a home on the hill past the little one room schoolhouse. Later, they lived in town in a small second floor apartment. After Ezra died, she went to live in the Masonic Home until her death.
N.C.D.

A small brass wind clock is all that we have to recall this memorable man and woman and the gracious position they *both* offered to accept during our early childhood years.

Photographer unknown
"*My music teacher, Mabel Morey.*" *N.C.D.*
circa early 1900's

Photo by Author

Note: As children, every birthday we would receive a card with a dollar in it.

MAN'S BATTLE with the INFLUENZA of 1918

The first wave of influenza was reported at Camp Funston, KS. on March 4, 1918. Eight days later, Nellie would be celebrating her sixth birthday. She and her brother were now living with their Aunt and Uncle on the hill, while her mother recouped at the Rome-Oneida Hospital for Tuberculosis. There were plans of Nellie beginning first grade at the small one room schoolhouse on the hill in the fall. Influenza hit the shores of Europe in early April as troopships docked in France. In May there were numerous reports of flu in Portugal and Spain. Soon it became known as the Spanish flu.

The second wave began in a little town called Brest, France on August 22. Soldiers began turning blue and dying just hours after exhibiting symptoms. The second assault began with a vengeance. The flu was quickly given the nickname of Purple Death.

Nellie and Aunt Catherine were busy getting outfits ready for Nellie's first day at school, totally unaware of what was just around the corner. Troopships docked in Boston, MA., Freetown and Sierra Leone, Africa with contagious soldiers. The United States had declared war on Germany and ships were traveling to all the remote places of the world. Servicemen and the flu docked in the Alaska Territory, Iceland, Samoa, New Zealand, and many other distant lands.

In Alaska, towns were surrounded by a line of red flags. Outsiders were not permitted past the markings. Cabins were built beyond the communities and furnished with food and the necessary supplies for traveling fisherman and trappers. Some villages sent armed guards several miles south of their villages to turn back anyone who might be carrying the lethal flu. In spite of this, entire villages were being wiped out. In Brevig, a small Inuit community of eighty, north of Nome, bodies were discovered in an igloo torn apart and eaten by sled dogs. Seventy-two villagers died. A few children were left for pick up.

The deadly flu made its way to Portsmouth, N.H., Newport, R.I., and Fort Devens (an army base thirty miles west of Boston). Pockets were showing up in Philadelphia, PA., Fort Dix, N.J. and Fort Meade, MD.

At the end of September the October draft was cancelled. Some military camps were placed under quarantine. In 1918, of the almost twenty million Americans that came

MAN'S BATTLE with INFLUENZA OF 1918 cont'd

down with the virus, half a million died. Those that died generally died from the complications of bacterial pneumonia for antibiotics had not yet been discovered.

In the United States, towns were being closed down. Residents were afraid and feeling a sense of helplessness. During World War I, out of every one hundred soldiers killed in battle, eighty-five were killed from flu.

By October 16, 1918, cities and communities were closing churches, schools, movie houses, theatres and asked not to hold funerals. In many of the big cities residents were asked to put boxes on porches and a cart would come by to pick them up. White flags flew outside the windows to denote the influenza. People treated at home often recovered better than residents admitted to hospitals. This increased their chances of catching bacterial pneumonia.

LETTER 11 *REMEMBERING the 1918 INFLUENZA*

I was six years old during the influenza epidemic. My memories were that many people died. My school teacher, Theresa Hammond died from it and many, many other friends. Theresa was in her twenties. To the best of my memory, she was single. Everyone was asked to stay apart. The flu arrived in upper New York State sometime in the autumn of 1918. I can remember being really sick — headache, temperature and vomiting etc. My brother was sick, too. His room was at the head of the stairs. My room was across the front of the house. My Aunt and Uncle were also extremely sick. They stayed in bed for two weeks. A doctor visited Aunt Catherine and Uncle Roswell while they had the flu. A male friend came each day to care for the animals and check on my brother, me and my Aunt and Uncle. When people died in those days, a wreath was hung on the front door. My music teacher and her husband (the Moreys) also lived on the hill above Aunt Catherine and Uncle Roswell's house. They got sick, too, but took care of each other.

I remember people talking about a huge dust cloud with a yellowish appearance that smelled bad. It began in the Midwest somewhere and worked its way across the country to the east coast. I do not remember the exact date. Some blamed it on the spread of the flu.   N.C.D.

"KEEP YOUR WINDOWS OPEN"
Signs by the Anti-Tuberculosis League were placed everywhere.

Illustration 2. Moon Hill

An early storm covered the ground with a deep layer of snow that fall. A black wreath hung on the door of Nellie's one room schoolhouse. The building went dark as the second wave of the pandemic continued. It was unrelenting through autumn of 1918.

1918 INFLUENZA cont'd   *THE THIRD WAVE*

November 11, 1918, at 11 a.m., Germany signed a general peace agreement to end the conflict. The end of World War I moved the Influenza Pandemic to the back pages of newspapers. It was now 1919. In actuality, the third wave of the pandemic had begun to circle the globe all over again. There were large death tolls in Paris, New York City and San Francisco. More graves to dig, but few took notice.

On April 3, 1919, President Woodrow Wilson became stricken, during the Paris Peace Conference. His temperature rose, his breathing was labored and he had a continuous cough. During the first twelve hours, his life was in obvious peril. He recovered though, but was forever weakened by the sickness and in September, 1919 suffered a disabling stroke. He served out the remainder of his office for all good purposes incapacitated.

Westmoreland, NY. 1998   Photo by Author

Back at the Rome-Oneida Tuberculosis Hospital, Nellie's mother, Ethel Elizabeth, already weakened from her long years of confinement, had contracted pneumonia and passed away on April 14, 1919. A funeral *was* held, but the three children did not go to the cemetery.

World War I was over. There were parades.   circa May 1919   RAD

Illustration 3. Third Wave Map of the 1918 Influenza

In 2013 over thirty-three percent of the world population is still infected with TB. That is one-third of our population. After many years of documentation for the illnesses that interrupt our lives every few decades or half century, names emerge such as: The Grippe, Influenza, Flu, Purple Death, Spanish Flu, Swine Flu, Bird Flu, Asian Flu, TB Plague, Black Death, HIV/Aids, Ebola, etc. and others not yet named.

"THE SARDINE SYNDROME" will continue to exist as long as animals for food are confined in unnatural, unclean, extreme living conditions (environments that encourage future pandemics). Humans also living in unsanitary, crowded conditions keep the rollercoaster of influenza continuing. Good hygiene can not be bought. Poor bathing habits and dubious sexual practices over thousands of years keep epidemics ongoing. A countries' *culture*, "if you will?"

SUGGESTED READING:

PURPLE DEATH By David Getz
THE GREAT INFLUENZA By John M. Barry
and Author of RISING TIDE
EPIDEMIC! By Stephanie True Peters

A window on "the hill"   Photographer unknown

Windows opened up all across the land, including the window opening onto the side porch of Aunt Catherine's farm house in 1919. Some were not sure whether the flu was being let in or out. A jump rope ditty was heard on many play yards: *"I had a bird and his name was Enza. I opened the window and in flew Enza"*

LETTER 12 *OUR ONE ROOM SCHOOLHOUSE*

The school covered grades one thru eight. There were eight students in my graduation class from eighth grade. One was my youngest brother, myself, Annie Edwards and Ruth and James Doyle...plus three others I can not remember. Some of my teachers were Theresa Hammond (lost to the 1918 influenza) and Mary Lewis Oberneser.

The school was located about 1 mile above Aunt Catherine's house.   N.C.D.

Illustration 4. One Room Schoolhouse

    Nellie loved her little schoolhouse, in spite of its shaky beginnings. She always remembered her first grade teacher named Miss Hammond.

NELLIE'S TALES

LETTER 13   *THE MAILMAN'S DAUGHTER*

The previous summer, the mailman's daughter got her leg caught in a wagon wheel and had to have it amputated. She was not playing with us, but Aunt Catherine did hear about it and forbid us from riding on a four-wheel gig. Our game was to get it started down the hill — then run and jump on. Now our little game was suddenly banned.

The next summer my brother and I were watching our school teacher walk down the field toward the valley like we always did. We got to playing with this wagon (two wheels on an axel). Of course, Nellie broke the rules and got her leg caught in the wheel and had to yell to her brother to stop the wheel. He did and saved my leg. I have a good sized scar to prove my story.

For many years, I told the story that my leg was caught in a barbed wire fence. The Dr. (while sewing up my damaged leg) kept mumbling to himself that he just couldn't believe that I could do that to myself in that manner. I had to receive a couple of needles in the stomach for tetanus. The scar was under my right knee. It was two and a half inches wide and three inches long.   N.C.D.

Upstate New York. circa early 1900's   Photographer unknown

LETTER 14   *THE HINDENBURG*

When I was in my twenties, Aunt Catherine and I visited the Hindenburg at the Utica Airport. It was not in a hanger, but out in the open. We saw Hitler, who was standing in the crowd.   N.C.D.

LETTER 15   *TOILETS*

In my childhood most toilets were located out of doors. This meant we made a trip from the house to an outdoor toilet no matter what the weather was like. I always felt that the real cold weather, many times, would give me a good excuse for putting off a trip to the bathroom!

Uncle Roswell, of course, would go many times in the barn where the cows went, while doing the chores. The ladies had to suffer the cold toilet seats.

X = BARN (left)
X = OUTSIDE TOILET

X = AUNT CATHERINE'S HOUSE (ninety feet from barn)

Photographer unknown
Nellie, Upstate NY circa 1900's

LETTER 16 *SKIING, SLEDDING and BASEBALL*

For recreation, during the winter months, we skied. My brother and I owned our skies and we could handle ourselves well. It was our favorite sport. We also liked sledding. We took our famous sled ride down Lewis' Hill just as Aunt Catherine and Uncle Roswell were returning back from buying groceries in the valley. We had to make it between two fence posts. Just as we started, I spotted the team of horses coming up the hill pulling the sled of groceries. We made it, but Aunt Catherine was screaming all the way — fearful that she would never get us raised without us killing ourselves first. This event took place in the early 1920's.

Nellie had two older brothers, **B**ernard and **C**hester, and during the summer months she had to play baseball with them. "I was a better ball player than they were," bragged Nellie. We named ourselves the team of **NBC** (from the TV station).   N.C.D.

NELLIE'S TALES cont'd

Playing London Bridge at the Stone House

Nellie (my Fair Lady) with her brothers and cousins. circa 1900's

LETTER 17 *A STONE HOUSE TALE*

One summer, my cousin and I got into a fight with two older boy cousins. They grabbed my dress by the hem and tore it badly. My cousin and I thought it was funny, but Aunt Catherine wasn't too pleased when she saw my dress.

We had a mad crush on a boy down the street, who was about five years older than we were. One afternoon the two of us conspired a plot to make the younger boys jealous. The boy down the street suggested that he drive by and have us jump into his car and he would speed off with us.   N.C.D.

The Stone House. circa early 1900's   Photographers unknown

Above is the Stone House that gave Nellie comfort growing up as a child. "Going to Grandpa and Grandma's house," she would say. The early family reunions were held without water and electricity. Before the home was purchased by E.J.C., the reunions were conducted at various relative's homes in the nearby area. Nellie's grandparents were determined to keep the family together.

Nellie was only sixteen years old when both her Dad's parents had passed away. The Stone House fell into disarray as it passed by several renters waiting for that "just right" family to move in.

LETTER 18   *A COUNTRY HORNING*

A horning is when everyone drove to a home where a recent wedding had taken place. The bride and groom were expected to prepare a snack and serve coffee and we all chatted and had fun.

Horning's are done after dark and after the recent bride and groom had gone to bed. The cars arrived with their head lights off. On signal, the lights would go on and horns would blare!!! This was an old country tradition.   N.C.D.

Photographer unknown

"Me and my oldest brother, Chet." N.C.D. circa early 1900's

PETS THROUGH THE YEARS

LETTER 19 *FAVORITE NAMES for HORSES MAUDE, JENNY and PRINCE*

Maude and Jenny were the two horses needed to pull the carriage at Aunt Catherine and Uncle Roswell's house on the hill. Maude was black spotted (dapple-grey) and Jenny was dark brown. Maude would only let me ride her.

In the barn we had a dairy of cows. Later, just one cow. Also, we had pigs and chickens. My brother had rabbits, chickens, ducks and sheep. He helped with all the animals and so did I.

Photographer unknown
Nellie, Jenny (the horse) and the free roaming chickens...1920's

LETTER 19 *NAMES for HORSES cont'd*

A STONE HOUSE HORSE

Prince was a tan horse with spots owned by Grandpa Elmer at the Stone House in New York State. Below, my oldest brother and cousins riding Prince. Grandpa Elmer is holding the reigns...circa early 1900's. N.C.D.

Photographers unknown

LETTER 20
FAVORITE PET DOGS...

LADDIE and SPORT

Laddie, the family dog at Aunt Catherine and Uncle Roswell's house on the hill (right), was a medium sized dog with long yellow hair. Jill asked, "Did you like him?" Nellie replied, "I sure did."

Sport, was my second dog. He was a great favorite, too. Sport was black and brown.

"My Aunt and Uncle with our dog Laddie." N.C.D. circa early 1900's

and a PET RABBIT

My brother had an "unnamed" pet rabbit he kept in the garage in a cage. N.C.D.

PETS THROUGH THE YEARS cont'd

LETTER 22 *FAVORITE NAMES for CATS*

BABE

One day many summers ago, Uncle Roswell was mowing grass with a cross-cut mower, and the grass was very tall. He accidentally cut off one of my cat's hind legs. The cat was missing close to a week.

Aunt Catherine and I were doing dishes in the kitchen. She was washing and I was drying. I was looking out the window that over looked our back lawn. All at once I realized that our cat was hobbling down our back lawn. I quickly called Aunt Catherine's attention to it. We went rushing to the back yard to find our mama cat had lost one of her hind legs. We picked her up and carried her into the house. We placed her on a towel in the kitchen, and gave her a large bowl of milk to drink. She quickly lapped it all up, for she had nothing to eat and little to drink for a week. She stayed there until she was completely healed. We had her for many more years and she even had kittens after that.

I vowed I would spend the rest of my life caring for her. Even Uncle Roswell would hold the screen door open for her so she could get in and out more easily. The mower was horse drawn and the cross bar went back and forth. Uncle Roswell did not see it happen and felt very bad.

Babe in Nellie's arms. circa mid-1920's   Photographer unknown

LETTER 22 *FAVORITE NAMES for CATS cont'd*
TABBY and STAR

Tabby and Star were my cats at Aunt Catherine and Uncle Roswell's house on the hill in Upstate New York.

Tabby and family with Nellie. 1930   Photographers unknown

Little Star. 1930

The hole in the right side of both photos is where I tacked them up in my dorm room when I went to college in 1930. Later they were placed in my scrapbook.   N.C.D.

REMEMBERING MY EARLY HOLIDAYS

LETTER 24   *THANKSGIVING*

"My much loved Aunt Ruth." N.C.D.   Photographer unkn

Weather permitting, Thanksgiving was a gathering time for the large extended families. As the fall leaves fell, horse and carriages would trek to the designated place of the fall feast. Thanksgiving was the time of year I could spend time with my Aunt Ruth. When I was twelve or thirteen years old, we had an earthquake at Aunt Catherine's house, circa mid-1920's. Aunt Ruth was there.   N.C.D.

> Aunt Ruth was a "stand out" in Nellie's life. Although unable to have any children of her own, Ruth married and was Postmaster in a small interior New York State town for many years. She was liked and highly respected. A lady renowned for her corn chowder soup.

LETTER 24   *EARLY CHRISTMASES*

Christmas trees didn't have electric bulbs on them for there wasn't any electricity. Only plain candles were snapped onto the tree. I was always concerned, as were

LETTER 24 *EARLY CHRISTMASES* cont'd

other family members, that the tree would catch fire and burn down our house I never removed my eyes from the lighted candles. The closest fire truck was a considerable distance away. This period of time was when I was in eighth grade on up through high school.

When I was younger, I remember Dad walking up the hill with a sack full of gifts for everyone. I remember my special Christmas gift from Dad was a sailor blouse when I was about twelve years old. Aunt Catherine played Christmas carols for the family to sing on the piano.   N.C.D.

LETTER 25 *PAST NEW YEAR'S EVES*

We usually spent New Year's Eve at home with the family playing cards and games. Aunt Catherine would prepare a midnight snack around 11:30 pm. At midnight we would each kiss each other and wish each other a Happy New Year. We all went out in the back yard and beat on pans!

One New Year's Eve, my brother took me down town when I was about eighteen. We went to the local theatre to celebrate. Their stage show was so risqué that my brother said, "Lets go back home." Aunt Catherine and Uncle Roswell were so pleased to see us, that Aunt Catherine immediately prepared a nice spread of food — "lunch" as Nellie put it. We spent the rest of New Year's Eve at home playing Pinochle and another card game (Pedro?) until midnight. We all had fun. My oldest brother was in town with Dad for that New Year's Eve.   N.C.D.

LETTER 26 *VALENTINE'S DAY*

When I was young, our teacher had us make Valentines in school to give to our parents. My mother would always send us handmade Valentines and candy. I don't recall that we necessarily wore red clothing like today.   N.C.D.

LETTER 27 *EASTER MEMORIES*

Many of our Easters were made happy by our favorite relatives Eloise and Roy visiting from Syracuse, New York. I really felt that they were very fond of my brother and myself and wanted to make our Easter very special. They

Letter 27 *EASTER MEMORIES cont'd*

always came laden with Easter goodies, such as chocolate bunnies and Easter baskets. They hid the baskets and my brother and I had to find them.

Dad and my oldest brother would also visit us at this time. Easter time the weather was normally chilly and sometimes downright cold with snow on the ground. My youngest brother would often receive a pet rabbit. Sometimes Uncle Roswell would prepare the rabbit for food later in the season.

N.C.D.

LETTER 28 *JULY 4th FIREWORKS*

Many times, our relatives from Syracuse would come to spend July 4th weekend with us. They would bring lots of firecrackers.

Aunt Catherine, Uncle Roswell and Bernard and I would sit in the yard while Roy would shoot off the firecrackers. Sometimes our older brother would join us.   N.C.D.

LETTER 29 *HALLOWEEN PRANKS*

Aunt Catherine didn't allow us to go out when we were younger. I remember once when we were in our teens that Aunt Catherine and Uncle Roswell went to Camden on Halloween to visit the Stone House on an anniversary date. They left my brother and me at home where we were suppose to stay. We ventured out wearing old clothes and walked around the neighborhood with a large brown paper bag. We collected candies from our neighbors. My brother and I pulled stockings over our heads and marched around all the nearby houses.

A Polish family lived above us and they were strict with their kids, too. We went around rapping on mailboxes. When the people came out of their homes, we ran. Sometimes bullets flew over our heads and we had to crawl in the ditches all the way home.

All three of us were culprits. We always did our pranks when Aunt Catherine and Uncle Roswell would visit the relatives at anniversary time in October.   N.C.D.

ERA of FIRSTS

LETTER 30   *ELECTRICITY COMES TO THE HILL*

I was in high school when Aunt Catherine and Uncle Roswell received electricity for the first time into their home. I was walking home from my school in the valley.
When I came to the brow of the hill, I could see our home with lights shining from top to bottom. Aunt Catherine had put all the lights on for me to see for the first time. The date was in the late 1920's. Before this time we only had kerosene lights to read by.   N.C.D.

LETTER 31   *FIRST TELEPHONE EXPERIENCES*

The phone hung on the wall and you had to crank it. Each household was given a number. Our first number was "2". The phone sounded two rings when someone was calling us. There were four or five families assigned to a line.

A favorite pastime for the ladies in the evening was to pick up the receiver and listen in on someone else's ring. Aunt Catherine, being hard of hearing, always said, "if they would just hang up, I could hear better." She was referring to her neighbors who would be listening in! My oldest brother used to get a big kick out of that.   N.C.D.

LETTER 32   *FIRST RADIO ENCOUNTER*

I remember the first radio we had. Aunt Catherine sat in the living room and listened to the afternoon shows. She thoroughly enjoyed them. She would prepare the evening meal vegetables while listening to the broadcasts.

It was during this time that Aunt Catherine taught me how to knit. This kept our hands busy while we listened to it. I totally enjoyed knitting scarves, mittens and sweaters, etc. I even knit myself a two piece skirt and blouse (aqua). I wore it while I was carrying all my children because it stretched as I grew larger.   N.C.D.

ERA of FIRSTS cont'd

LETTER 33   *OUR FIRST MODEL-T*

It was summertime and in those days no licenses were required. Uncle Roswell went to town to drive our new Model-T home. He paid $400.00 for the car.

Aunt Catherine and I were standing at the back door when Uncle Roswell shot by us with his shirt wringing wet with sweat. He had a corn cob pipe in his mouth. He had driven the car though town traffic, up the Hill and into the circular drive without any training.   N.C.D.

LETTER 34   *MY FIRST DENTIST*

My first dentist was the one my Aunt Catherine and Uncle Roswell went to and he was very competent. They used Novocain at that time, if needed. A good dentist was hard to come by in the wooded interior of New York State during the early years.

At eighty-six years old, I still have all my teeth, except for my four wisdom teeth. I presently have no cavities.

N.C.D.

LETTER 35   *MY FIRST PLANE RIDE*

While on a visit to the local airport, Aunt Catherine almost let me take a ride in an airplane. She opened her purse and took out $4.00 — thought a moment — then tucked the $4.00 back in her purse. She decided she wasn't going to chance letting me go up in a plane for a ride. I was just as pleased! I was in my early teens as best I can remember.

N.C.D

"LINDY" AND HIS SMILE

Courtesy of a local newspaper, Lindy and his smile made his way into Nellie's scrapbook. In 1927, Charles Lindbergh made the first solo non-stop flight across the Atlantic from Long Island to Paris in the Spirit of St. Louis.

NELLIE'S SCRAPBOOK

Photographers unknown
In the background can be seen the wagon wheel of her childhood days...the wheel Nellie had caught her leg in.

Nellie practiced and practiced for those coveted scholarships, circa late 1920's.

Grandpa Elmer came to live with Aunt Catherine briefly after his wife Mary Amelia died. He did not like listening to Nellie practice the trumpet, so she moved in temporarily with Mr. and Mrs. Morey in the valley. Elmer Jay passed away less than two months after the death of his wife in 1928.

Nellie at the University circa early 1930's

During her University years she took on a *"Meryl Steep"* (the actress) kind of look. Nellie graduated from Rochester University with the honor of being the first female trumpet major in the Eastman School of Music.

Nellie circa early 1930's

33

NELLIE'S SCRAPBOOK cont'd

Circa early 1930's — Photographers unknown

A warm, but anti-climatic spring brought on Nellie's college graduation. The Eastman School of Music was now behind her and so was the flutter of social life she had enjoyed.

Nellie acquired the noble job of teaching music at the Newington Home for Crippled Children.

Nellie returns to the "hill"...

Weddings began and bouquets were tossed...

The winds of time were blowing...Nellie was no longer a very young girl...*though every dream remembered well from girlhood's shimmering days*...she now must prepare for spring's departure and plan for summer's ways. Nellie was twenty-seven. Many of her friends were putting down roots and having children of their own, including her younger brother.

CHAPTER II
RANDOLPH MEETS NELLIE

Randolph had returned from the Alaska Territory just over two and a half years ago. He had traveled over 5,500 miles to the rugged outposts of interior Alaska to search for gold.

On his return, he met again with his prospector friends in Pineville, North Carolina. Maybe he could talk them into returning to Alaska with him — for he had located some pretty choice places. How could he describe this land of wonder *"above the 60,"* as Alaskans put it? Photographs? Unfortunately, the images of yesterday are not what they are today — and his words could not adequately express the awe he had just witnessed. Randolph took a cooldown at the Gold Bug Mining Camp in North Carolina. He mined there for a while, but something was still not right.

Gold Bug Mining Camp, NC.
March, 1937   Photos by RAD

RAD panning for gold at Gold Bug Mine. April 25, 1937

Gold Bug Mine, NC — 50 ft. sluice box

Randolph eventually resigned himself to the reality of the world and settled into job hunting. With a little help, he was offered a job in upstate New York.

Randolph Angus Douglas met Nellie up on the hill. He had acquired a room at Aunt Catherine's house while working at his job in the valley. Aunt Catherine was now running a boarding house, renting out some of her rooms. Nellie and Randolph dated for three months, then wed. Together they had three children and were married for over forty-five years.

Randolph and Nellie — Photographer unknown

LETTER 36 *OUR WEDDING*
December fourteenth

The wedding was held at Aunt Catherine's house on a rolling hill in upstate New York. The ceremony took place in the living room in front of the fireplace.

It was an evening wedding in the beginning of winter. Aunt Catherine and Uncle Roswell hired some friends to cater the reception indoors. Interestingly, Uncle Roswell and Aunt Catherine's anniversary was December fifteenth. One day apart.

My two brothers were suppose to help with the reception. My younger brother was very helpful. He greeted and sat the guests. My older brother, on the other hand, chatted with his friends and enjoyed the refreshments.

The day of the wedding there was snow and ice on the ground. Cars got stuck on the hill. Dad and I arrived early to make sure we made it on time!

LETTER 36 *OUR WEDDING* cont'd

Nellie continued, the wedding party consisted of the maid of honor, my youngest brother's first wife. Bridesmaids were my high school music teacher, and two college friends. The flower girl was my first niece. She wore a blue dress. Randolph's brother was best man. Our minister was the minister of the First Presbyterian Church in the valley. Randolph's nephew, drove Randolph's father up with him from central New Jersey.

My music teacher played the piano and my college friend sang solos. My other college friend, played a violin solo. My wedding dress was purchased in the valley.   N.C.D.

> Mr. and Mrs. Roswell D. Ripley
>
> announce the marriage of their neice
>
> Nellie Elizabeth
>
> to
>
> Randolph Angus Douglas
>
> on
>
> Saturday, the fourteenth of December

The author noted that Nellie's unbroken recollection of her wedding was reiterated with a constant sparkle in her eye. She recalled every detail with great delight.

Now their previous lives will truly be history, a place in their pasts. They must decide what to do with all of their newly acquired interests in common. What parts of their lives will they leave behind and what parts will they take with them to their new home together? A farewell of sorts.

Photographer unknown
"Our northern New Jersey home." N.C.D. circa mid-1940's

Nellie began putting down her own roots in an "over wintered" upper New York State town close to her Aunt and Uncle.

Nellie's two daughter's had already arrived when a job opportunity opened up and a move to northern New Jersey was perhaps predestined. A modest cottage was purchased and soon her family was complete. Three in all.

It was in this cottage kitchen, while brushing her oldest daughter's hair that she expressed something insightful. "Someday a man on a white horse will ride up and take you away from me," she said. Nellie was right and I would like to dedicate this book to him.

As time went on Nellie's music began to call. There was a strong desire to pass on her hard worked for music education to future generations...

Photograph by Author

and, another location had to be considered.

Photographer unknown

A new location chosen. NJ, circa early 1950's
Note: Look very carefully to see the flag flying in the side yard.

Nellie happily taught music and they raised their "fifties kind of family" in northern New Jersey, as the years came and went. A Chapter not written, but life lived to its fullest.

LETTER 37 *OUR FIRST BLACK and WHITE TV*

The first black and white TV experience was in our new northern New Jersey town in the mid-1950's. "Some good friends of ours bought the first black and white TV in town. I taught their three sons piano lessons, said Nellie.

We spent many enjoyable evenings having supper at their house. The children would watch the little black and white TV set in the living room while we chatted in the dining room. When they came to our house, the younger set would play Randolph's new *"Gold Bug Game,"* inspired from his trip to Alaska. Some time later, we invested in a black and white TV set of our own.   N.C.D.

OUR 1950'S FAVORITE TV SERIES LIST
(Below) Nellie points out what her "Fifty's Family" watched and listened to:

Lassie (1954-1973) Radio (1947-1950)
Father Knows Best (1954-1960) Radio (1949 - 1952)
The Gene Autry Show (1950-1956) Radio (1940-1956)
The Honeymooners (1951-1952) The Cavalcade of Stars as a 6 minute sketch, then to CBS (1952-1956) where the "classic 39" episodes were aired

1950'S FAVORITE TV SERIES LIST cont'd

Leave it to Beaver (1957-1963)
The Jack Benny Show (1954-1958) Radio (first appeared in 1932)
The Twilight Zone (1959-1964)
My Little Margie (1952-1955)
Dennis the Menace (1959-1963) originating from Hank Ketcham's comic strip of the same name, launched March 12, 1951.
The Ed Sullivan Show (1948-1971)
Sergeant Preston of the Yukon (1955-1958) Radio (1947-1950)
Wagon Train (NBC 1957-1962) (ABC 1962-65)
Alfred Hitchcock Presents (1955-1962) A. H. directed many of the episodes
Gunsmoke (1955-1975)
The Lone Ranger (1949-1957) Radio (1933) Comic strip (1938-1971) films and novels followed including a comic book.
I've Got a Secret (1952-1967) family game show
The Millionaire (1955-1960)
Sky King (1940-1950's) Radio and television series
The Red Skelton Show (1951-1971) Radio (1941-1953)
My Friend Flicka (1955-1958)
The Life of Riley (1953-1958)
To Tell the Truth (1956-1958)
This is Your Life Ralph Edwards…..Radio (1948-1952) …Host (1952-1961)
Mr. Peepers (1952-1955)
The George Gobel Show (1954-1960)
What's My Line? (1950-1967)
Annie Oakley (1954-1956)
Bonanza (1959-1973)
Tombstone Territory (1957-1959)
The Invisible Man (1958-1959)
The Thin Man (1957-1959)
The Perry Como Show (1949-1963) later…..Host The Kraft Music Hall (till 1967)
Dragnet (1951-1959) Radio (1949-1957)
Sea Hunt (1958-1961)…Host (1962-1992)
The Adventures of Ozzie and Harriet (1952-1966)
Death Valley Days (1952-1975)

1950'S FAVORITE TV SERIES LIST cont'd

The Adventures of Rin Tin Tin (1954-1960's)
　　The original Rin Tin Tin (dog) was born in France during a time of War in the mid-1920's. His owner brought him to the United States and soon the dog was noticed by Warner Brothers with the help of his aggressive, but adoring owner (agent). A movie called "Where the North Begins," was released successfully by the fledgling Warner Brothers Studio. Rin Tin Tin's career was off and running. He even did the Vaudeville circuit with other stars. The original Rin Tin Tin died in 1932.
　　The Rin Tin Tin saga continued through his off spring. A TV series began in 1954 and Rin Tin Tin the XXII is now the spokes dog for the American Humane Society and recently presided over the ringing at the New York Stock exchange.

Life and Legend of Wyatt Earp (1955-1961)
Desilu Productions
　　A Wyatt Earp's bio: *Frontier Marshal* came out in 1931. Several motion pictures followed from silent film to present day...and the legend continues on. Actors who have filled Wyatt's boots were: Hugh O'Brian, James Garner, Will Greer, Joel McCrea, Randolph Scott, Kevin Costner, Richard Dix, Kurt Russell, Henry Fonda and Leo Gordon.

Our northern New Jersey home. circa mid-1950's　　Photographed by Author

1950's FAVORITE TV SERIES LIST cont'd

Some of the movies (internet movie database) include: Hour of the Gun, Sunset, The Life and Legend of Wyatt Earp, Wyatt Earp: Return to Tombstone, The Guns of Paradise and The Gambler Returns: The Luck of the Draw.

The Roy Rogers Show (1951-1957)
The Ed Sullivan Show (1948-1971)
My Friend Irma (1952-1954)
Our Miss Brooks (1952-1957) Radio (1948-1957)
Wonderful World of Disney Walt Disney Host (1954-1966)
The Howdy Doody Show (1954-1959)
The Jimmy Durante Show (1954-1957)
The Bob Cummings Show (1955-1959)
The Adventures of Wild Bill Hickok (1951-1958)
Death Valley Days (1952-1975)
Tales of Wells Fargo (1957-1962)
Show of Shows Sid Cesar and Imogene Coca (1950-54)
Imogene Coca Show (1954-1955)
Maverick (1957-1962)
The Northwest Passage (1958-1959)
The State Troopers (1956-1959)
Candid Camera In the mid-fifties, for the first time live performances of reality TV began appearing. Shows like Candid Camera. The audience loved it...reality TV was born.

ABC World News (1953 thru present day)
CBS Evening News (1948 thru present day)
NBC Nightly News (1940 thru present day)

NBC has had many logos through the years, dating back to radio in the 1930's. First, a bolt of lightning with variations, then a Television Camera, an Xylophone with a mallet and finally the famed Peacock — begun in the 1950's to denote colored television.

I Remember Mama live (1949-1956) several screenings between these years have been donated by various sources, but other unrecorded episodes are mostly lost. Twenty-six filmed episodes *are* in a storage facility in New Jersey.

1950's FAVORITE TV SERIES LIST concludes
EPISODES

The importance of TV episodes being stored properly for posterity is comparable to the preserving of great works of art, the maintaining of distinguished motion pictures, or the safe guarding of notable books through the past centuries.

The number of episodes in a particular TV series varies, many times seeming longer because of reruns, but each one has a history all its own. Most of the series had a surprisingly short duration of run time.

It is essential to record history as accurately as possible for our future generations. These episodes are a time capsule of our past and the way we were — true treasures.

Empty garage. circa late 1980's   Photograph by Author

Nellie's husband of forty-five years passed away in the late 1980's. She lived in the house alone for a couple of years before selling the house and moving into a local apartment to be by her friends. Though, as the moments passed on Nellie finally realized it was time to move closer to one of her family members, families that had long since scattered. Nellie decided to relocate, at least for a while, to Nashville, Tennessee, bringing her closer to her youngest daughter and her family. After all, Nashville *was* the city of music. Holidays came and went as Nellie enjoyed her Tennessee families.

Approximately three years later, however, the lure of thriving in the Florida sunshine became most appealing when the invite came in to live down in Florida with her oldest daughter, Jill and her husband, Emory.

BEACH HOUSE DAYS

The Jersey Shore. circa early 1960's   Photographer unknown

Beach houses were always the highlight of many summers, but as Nellie grew older...gradually they stopped.

Photo by Author
Alison and Diane enjoying the ocean breezes. circa late 1990's

Nellie could be heard singing "September Song" while playing the piano in at her TN. apartment and later from the back room of our Florida home. *"Oh, it's a long, long while from May to December, but the days grow short when you reach September."* Composed by Kurt Weill, with lyrics by Maxwell Anderson. Originally introduced by Walter Huston in the 1938 musical *Knickerbocker Holiday*.

CHAPTER III
LIFE'S DIRECTIONS

It was June 28, 1997. Several years had past since Nellie had relocated to Nashville from New Jersey. Nellie was eighty-five years old when we knocked on her apartment door at the Maybelle Carter Retirement Center in Nashville, Tennessee. Suitcase in hand, wearing the same outfit she had on the night before, Nellie was ready to join us in Florida and begin a new chapter in her life. We had invited her to live with us.

The city of music would soon be in our rearview mirror, as would the fond memories of all those she would be leaving behind. Each of her three children were fortunate to have some special last moments with her before her life concluded.

Nellie positioned herself intently on the edge of the back seat just behind ours, as she watched the long driveway of Maybelle Carter pass before her. A final photograph was taken and Nellie was fastened in for the highways of Tennessee, Georgia and Florida.

Maybelle Carter, Nashville, TN. 1997   Photograph by Author

Nellie arrives at her new home in Florida a few days later.

LADY NELLIE?

Lady Nellie of Titusville? 1997 Photograph by Author

WELCOME HOME NELLIE was written on a sign over the window in her FL. bedroom. Nellie was very excited to see her new digs. Her whirlwind life was just beginning. A new world awaited Nellie in the Sunshine State. It would be a lighter, brighter, faster world than she was accustomed to. A short lived, second wind, if you will. The environment she had spent a lifetime in was no longer there. Her husband had died, her music studio was closed and her children were grown with families of their own. She left many friends behind in New Jersey, but many were just no longer there. It was a lonely world, but Nellie was a good sport. She flew to New York to attend her beloved Stone House reunion, just one more time. This was accomplished with the assistance of relatives and friends. Would Nellie have preferred not to have gone? Not on your life and was very quick to respond to my question, "When did the reunion begin, anyway?" Nellie sat up straight and clearly answered, "To the best of my recollection the first family reunion at the (Norton) Stone House began in 1948 — that would be almost fifty years."

THE GOLDEN THREAD

In actuality, the first reunion at the Stone House was held many years earlier on July 19, 1926 with a newspaper article to prove it. Nellie was only fourteen years old. Her Grandparents entertained a family gathering bringing together the lineal descendents of Jeremiah Clarke (the emigrant American ancestor and former Governor of R. I. in 1648). Through Jeremiah, the family traces back to Edward I — King of England in 1272 and his daughter Princess Joan of Acre born in 1272.

The golden thread continues through Princess Joan's fourth child, Elizabeth. Eventually, weaving all the way back to William the Conqueror — first Norman King of England in 1066 and Alfred the Great — King of Wessex in 871. The old 1926 newspaper article concluded with Charlemagne — the fist emperor of the Western Roman Empire in 800.

In 1947, Elmer's grandson, Roger and his young family decided to make this their home. Soon after electricity and water were established, the reunions began again.

Nellie took her "fifties family" to this reunion every August. Children came running from the picnic grounds for that celebrated "jeep ride" by Roger Norton. The jeep would bump over the back roads of the Norton homestead while children screamed and laughed.

Also, there was the legendary "bear hunt" led by Nellie's post Alaska prospector husband, Randolph Angus Douglas. Oh, those were the days to be young.

In 2005, the summer after Nellie had passed away, the best way to remember her was to go back to the area she had frequented. Upon leaving, I will not forget looking back seeing Elaine and her daughter Mary, waving goodbye, knowing this would be the last time we would be attending. The annual gathering soon would be coming to a quiet close.

Photographs by Author
Keepers of the reunion.

NELLIE'S SCRAPBOOK cont'd

LETTER 38 *ABOUT CHILDBIRTH*

In the early forties, doctors would give you medication for pain if you asked for it. Even today, if women prefer to have natural childbirth, they can — but if the pain gets to be too tough, you can ask the Dr. for a painkiller. Regret having children? Absolutely not!

Children are <u>most important!</u> Today's women are very fortunate, because they can have them when ever they want them. Children are the essence of living. N.C.D.

LETTER 39 *POT OF GOLD*

The day our first daughter was born, my husband, Randy said, *"I traveled all the way to Alaska hunting for my pot of gold — only to find it in the golden red curls on our baby girl's head."* N.C.D.

LETTER 40 *BABY'S FIRST RIDE*

All of my children were born in fall months and each was like my first all over again. N.C.D.

When I took my babies out upon the quiet streets, the autumn leaves whirled all about, and rustled 'neath my feet. The melancholy shrubs were tinged with winter's bitter dyes.
Above, the clouds were sable-fringed, for autumn rode the skies.
When I wheeled my babies, I could feel the breath of spring. For like a bud, enchantingly, my babies were blossoming."
By Anne Campbell (from Nellie's scrapbook)

Jill and Nellie on porch of Oneida Lake Motel. 1997   Photo by U.E H

Evergreen Cemetery   LOCATING MY BROTHER

Upstate New York   Photograph by Author

After a stop by Oneida Lake in August, 1997, we drove east to locate the Evergreen Cemetery where Nellie's Mom (Ethel Elizabeth), Dad (Homer Jay), sister (Alice Mabel) and her "Aunt" Nellie were resting. It was situated in Westmoreland, New York. When Mom walked by and noticed Bernard's grave, on our way to the far side of the cemetery, she was taken back and uttered, *"Why there's Bernie!"* I do

not believe she had seen it before. For a moment, it was like an arrow had gone through her heart. He was her beloved brother, Bernard. The one who shared all the events of her earlier life. I realized then, that they were as "one" in those early days. The **B** in NBC was now gone.

Soon, Nellie's older brother, Chester (the **C**), would pass on— and a few years later the **N,** too, was gone, but their little game of **NBC** can always be thought of as long as there is an **NBC** television network.

Photographer unknown
"Me and my brother" N.C.D. *early1920's*

ORANGES

Nellie picking oranges. 1997   Photograph by Author

Back in Florida Nellie picked oranges in our backyard with a smile as constant as the Florida sunshine. A simple pleasure Nellie enjoyed, that and gator hunting across the bridge with Emory and a flashlight. *"Seeing the gator's red eyes staring back at you is a real thrill,"* Nellie said. She was always eager to take a trip over the bridge to look for some more gators.

While picking oranges one afternoon, she commented that the United States sent oranges to Britain during World War II. *"They sent them to the Royal family,"* she said.

Curious, I asked her where she was when the news of Pearl Harbor broke. She said, *"I first heard the news of Pearl Harbor while we were living in the valley in upstate New York, just a little over two months after you were born."*

Photograph by Author

Long lines at Barnes and Noble. Orlando, FL. 1997

Photographer unknown

Jill, Nellie and President Jimmy Carter, Orlando, FL. 1997

President Carter allowed picture taking at his book signing in Orlando, FL. He had written several children's books illustrated by his daughter, Amy Carter. We were both thrilled to have our books autographed by someone of his standing.

ABOUT SPACE TRAVEL

Photograph by Author
A crowd watches Discovery launch from a pier in Titusville, Florida. 1998

LETTER 41 *ABOUT SPACE TRAVEL*

Regarding John Glenn going into space for the second time at age seventy-seven, he is qualified to go, if he wants to. At seventy-seven years old, it will give them a chance to see how an older person will hold up in space travel.

I think John Glenn's flight on Discovery will show senior citizens that there is much they can accomplish in later years. I feel I am lucky to be in Titusville, Florida where I can watch the launch in person. It is really historic.   N.C.D.

Note:
Lift off for John Glenn's flight on Discovery is a big event at the Kennedy Space Center, FL. and around the world. He soon will be the oldest man in space.

Nellie in Titusville, FL. 1998   Photograph by Author

Excitement builds as we all await the launch of the shuttle Discovery and John Glenn's second trip into space.

A witch windsock hangs to the left of Nellie's head indicating the season.

ABOUT SPACE TRAVEL cont'd

Photograph by Author
Discovery lift off, Titusville, FL. October 29, 1998
John Glenn's second flight into space.

Nellie's great grandson, Wyatt. 2010

Photograph by Author

　　Several years later, after viewing the second to last Discovery launch from the Kennedy Space Center, we too, toured the visitor center and contemplated what it would be like to travel into space, or walk on a distant planet.

　　On July 21, 2011, I was finishing the last few pages of *Nellie's Hill,* while high above ground, a group of astronauts were preparing to land the Shuttle Atlantis. This would be NASA's last shuttle mission. Upon its return from the International Space Station, Atlantis like the other three will go into permanent retirement.

　　The world watched as a little boy on TV poised to be interviewed in his *orange-red astronaut jump suit* by a British news reporter. Many excited visitors stood by at the visitor center at KSC in Florida and waited for the reporter as he asked his question to the young boy, "What would you like to be when you grow up?"...the boy went silent and could not answer. Dreaming of exploring the vastness of the universe has been a part of our childhood psyche through most of the 20th century and loosing the shuttle comes with much regret, but then there is Orion, those asteroids and that red planet they keep talking about — a n d what about the strange portals that keep showing up on Wyatt's drawings!!!

ABOUT SPACE TRAVEL concluded

NASA'S shuttle fleet can now be viewed around the country.

DISCOVERY at the Smithsonian, WA. DC

ATLANTIS at KSC, FL.

ENDEAVVOR at CA. Science Center, LA.

ENTERPRISE at Air and Space Museum, NYC

CHALLENGER lost after lift off. 1986

COLUMBIA disintegrated during re-entry. 2003

Nellie's great granddaughter, Erin views the last Discovery launch with mom, Yi-Pei. 2011

Photographs by Author

"Bird watchers" from all over the world, Titusville, FL. 2011

BEACH HOUSE DAYS

Nellie and granddaughter, Heather. Jersey Shore, 1998   Photo by Author

THE LAST BEACH HOUSE
By Heather Van Arsdel

Well, its hard to remember, but I do recall the very last beach house Grandma Nellie rented. It was called the "Butterfly House" and was in walking distance to the Barnegat Lighthouse. There was a long stone jetty out into the Atlantic Ocean. Yes, Grandma walked out there, too.

Grandma was always fun to be with because she would go along with whatever we came up with — all the while, keeping an infectious smile on her face. She loved playing cards, so we spent long evenings finishing card games before turning out the lights.

THE LAST BEACH HOUSE cont'd

The Butterfly House, Barnegat Light, NJ. 1998   Photographs by Author

One thing I always looked forward to as a young girl were the summers we vacationed at the beach. I would get to see my cousins and my Aunts and Uncle that we rarely got to see — many times all staying under one roof.

I remember one beach visit where we woke up one morning and the shore was lined with smelly, dead fish. I'm not sure what happened, but the story we heard from locals was that a fishing net broke loose in heavy seas. Later giving the house the nickname of "Sea Maggot." The silver lining to that was that the large waves also washed ashore all these really cool sea shells. Our much loved Aunt Elizabeth was visiting that week so we all went out shell hunting. To my surprise, I came upon a sand dollar in perfect condition. I still have it to this day...and, for our endless "free" entertainment there was a waist measuring contest between my mom and her sister. I think all families should have beach house adventures. Someday I will rent "King of the Dune."

Nellie and Emory. No training wheels, N. J. 1998

CHAPTER IV
PREPARING for a ROAD TRIP

Northern New Jersey. 1998   A neighbor's photo

One day, Nellie received some photos in the mail of her old New Jersey house, but the home in northern Jersey where Nellie raised her "fifties family" looked different now. The large fir trees in front of the house where her children once climbed were coming down. Nellie must have realized in viewing this photo that *her* century of living was coming to a close and there wasn't any thing she could do to halt it.

The cross country-road trip to Seattle, WA. was never more appealing than at this time. Nellie was eager to prepare and our early camping trips began in earnest. The rig below was used through October, 1998.

Photograph by Author

PREPARING for a ROAD TRIP cont'd

Nellie, Bryson City, N.C. 1997   Photograph by Author

Early camping trips had already begun. Numerous visits to the Smokey Mountains National Park were made — off our original camper, truck and dog, Sam would go.

After Nellie's arrival a fall leaves camping trip was made to N.C. and Nellie walks through the "Tunnel to Nowhere."

Nellie and the Author. Camping, circa 1997-98   Photograph by UEH

Another weekend we camped up in Ormond Beach, FL. to see the Fairchild Oak.

HALLOWEEN
HOUSE of SCREAMS

Another Halloween on the way and our camping adventures continue. A favorite spot in Central Florida was chosen for the dark day of Halloween. To avoid some local trick or treating, Diane decided to join us for a trip up to Silver Springs and a walk thru the *House of Screams*. Nellie was all for it. She loved Silver Springs.

It was very dark that evening and the crowd was particularly mischievous. We were having fun though, waiting in line for the *House of Screams,* until out from behind the bushes came the evil man with the python snake around his neck. He, too, seemed demonized as he headed straight for Nellie. His snake, also demonized, made a lunge. "He just wanted to say hello," the man said. It shook Nellie up and Emory had to sit with her while Diane and I went through the *House of Screams,* which was appropriately frightening.

One must remember back to when Nellie was an impish little girl playing tricks on *her* neighbors, while her Aunt and Uncle were away.

The evening was commemorated with a photograph in a photo booth. Barely fitting into the small area, the machine snapped and the following picture was captured below.

Three in a pix booth, Silver Springs, FL. Camping 1997-98

PREPARING for a ROAD TRIP cont'd

The "new" camper. 1998   Photographer unknown

In October we purchased a larger camper. This one had bunk beds that did not go unnoticed by Nellie.

Oh what a beautiful sight when it finally backed into place and the new gate was closed. This brought to reality the fact we were fast moving towards our goal of crossing the country and eventually camping up in Alaska.

A Pigeon Forge, TN. campground. 1998   Photograph by Author

We practiced our camping skills locally and on up to Tennessee for some Christmas camping. This was the "camper's" first experience with below freezing conditions. It passed. This Coachman Catalina was a three season 30- foot camper. Soon a Ford 250 diesel 4X4 truck was purchased to eventually tow it to Alaska and beyond.

Upon returning to Florida, we camped every chance we could, taking on the state east, west, north and south.

In mid September, 1999, Hurricane Floyd arrived and there was a mandatory evacuation ordered for our area. Hurricanes and travel trailers do not get alone well. This was our new Alaska-bound camper and we were not going to let Floyd catch up with it.

On Monday morning we boarded up the house, grabbed some important things and left town before the crowds set in. Nellie found all the activity very exciting. Stats on Floyd were a Category 5, 155 MPH /121 MB. It was heading right for Cape Canaveral. The Kennedy Space Center sent everyone home and Disney closed for the first time ever.

The hurricane was predicted to follow the Florida east coast north, possibly making landfall around Jacksonville. We pulled the camper west on I-10 along with many, many others. Soon after Tallahassee, it became bumper to bumper in what seemed about three hours of extremely heavy, desperate traffic. Finally, we arrived at our arranged western Florida panhandle campground. We gave Diane (Nellie's granddaughter who lived in Central Florida) a call on our cell and she kept us informed of the TV updates. Hopefully we will not find a lot of damage when we return and we did not.

The Styrofoam plate below is all that was available to sketch out our stay at this friendly, "end of the line" campground in the western Florida panhandle.

Illustration 5. Styrofoam Art. 1999

PREPARING for a ROAD TRIP cont'd

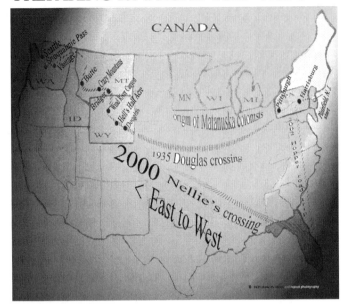

Illustration 6. Road trip map E to W

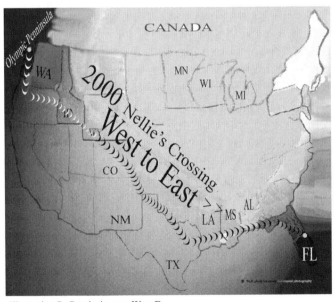

Illustration 7. Road trip map W to E

Alison in Florida. 1990's Photograph by Author

Remarks by Alison M. Van Arsdel
Paraphrased and revised from *Last Chance Alaska*

"My Mom (Jill), Stepdad (Emory) and Grandma (Nellie) are traveling across the country in an RV." Mom was dedicating herself to the adventure of following in her father's footsteps to retrace some old photos he had taken on a trip to Alaska to hunt for gold in 1935. It was our little source of bragging, that the three of them were "cool" and active in their retirement years.

I knew my Grandmother Nellie for thirty-four years before she passed away. Her first cross-country road trip at age eight-eight was truly remarkable, as we heard about it through phone calls and postcards along the way.

No journey is a wasted one. We profit most by allowing ourselves to live and do even that which might at first seem frightening or even improbable. We benefit by taking chances and knowing just when to change directions.

Shuttle Atlantis, Titusville, FL. 2000   Photograph by Author

A spectacular send-off, as the shuttle Atlantis arches over the blooming century plant in our front yard just before beginning our road trip across country (and on to Alaska). This was Emory's final launch at KSC before retirement.

CHAPTER V
NELLIE'S CROSSING

A century plant blooms, Titusville, FL. 2000 Photograph by Author

The Millennium New Year, 1999-2000 had just passed. Changing centuries is a big deal. The end of the world could be coming, computers could crash — in another words, jitters had taken over our planet.

However, the century plant continued to blossom, a Mockingbird perched on an upper left branch watches the world go by and we go on packing for our long journey west.

NELLIE'S CROSSING cont'd

The century plant and the cross-country travelers, Titusville, FL. 2000

A self-timer portrait was taken in Titusville, FL., before the East-West crossing began. On July 1, 2000 Emory, Jill, Nellie, Little Jon (dog), new truck and new camper posed for a photograph before beginning the demanding cross- country adventure. What could go wrong?

A couple of nights before we reached Paducah, Kentucky, Emory put regular gas in his diesel truck by mistake. Realizing his error, he quickly siphoned the gas into four jerry cans of five gallons each and when we reached Paducah he turned it into the nearest fire station. This town in Kentucky was especially interesting and our first exploratory stop since beginning the voyage. We headed right to the Ohio River. There were many old buildings with unusual architecture. The waterfront had rows and rows of well-painted murals.

On July 4, 2000, we arrived at the St. Louis Arch — Gateway to the West. It was 2 pm Central time when Nellie blurted out, "It's hotter than a Dutchman's love." Although, I am not sure how she knew that.

Nellie and Emory, St. Louis, MO. 2000   Photograph by Author

Little Jon (dog), in Iowa. 2000   Photograph by Author

We arrived at our cornfield campground in Iowa — where Nellie was *no* stranger. She had grown up around corn fields and seemed to enjoy the environment. After visiting with Emory's two brothers and their families, we turned the truck north toward the South Dakota border.

The weather was hot, but clear and good for travel. Off to the Badlands of South Dakota — Nellie's favorite place. On July 7, 2000, we drove the twenty mile loop and did a wheelchair stroll with Nellie and L. J. on an isolated trail out into the Badlands.

NELLIE'S CROSSING cont'd

Our rig in the Badlands of South Dakota. 2000   Photographs by Author

With the sun setting, in all this stunning desolation, we were all very thankful to have a brand new truck and camper. The weather was holding — still clear and hot.

Badlands National Park, S. D. 2000

Nellie's scar revealed. S. D. 2000   Photographs by Author

On July 7th, we came across the same type wagon that Nellie had caught her leg in as a child. This stop was before arriving at Mount Rushmore in South Dakota. Nellie revealed a very large, obvious scar from her earlier days.

The wagon. Rest stop in S. D. 2000

NELLIE'S CROSSING cont'd

Mount Rushmore National Memorial, S. D. 2000   Photograph by Author

GOLD

After gold was discovered in the Black Hills in 1874, prospectors, merchants and settlers poured into the Sioux Territory. A culture clash ensued leading to the atrocity of Wounded Knee on the morning of Dec. 29, 1890 — the bloodiest and final massacre in that area.

Approximately thirty years after Wounded Knee and fifty years from the discovery of gold in the Black Hills, Gutzon Borglum was contracted to begin work on the Mountain of Presidents (as it was known). After financing was established primarily through Government sources, the work eventually began. It was completed in 1941. This was also the year Borglum passed away. Gutzon had earlier completed the Stone Mountain Monument in GA.

Nellie enjoyed the outing to Mount Rushmore. She liked her Presidents.

Crazy Horse Memorial. July 8, 2000   Photographs by Author

That same day and just a short distance away we drove to the Crazy Horse Memorial. It was still under construction and totally dependent upon private donations. Crazy Horse has turned into a folk hero, as the man that fought against Indian relocation in the 1800's. Crazy Horse fiercely wanted to hold onto the ways of his people, but also realized the inevitable ending that was close at hand. He was a visionary that saw beyond the confines of his life.

Nellie found the museum most intriguing, especially when she found out Crazy Horse's second wife was named "Nellie."

Crazy Horse. July 8, 2000

73

NELLIE'S CROSSING cont'd

An Ice Age mammoth viewed by Nellie. 2000   Photographed by UEH

This ongoing paleontological dig site in Hot Springs, South Dakota is the largest in the world. As of 2013, sixty-one Ice Age mammoths have been found, fifty-eight Columbian mammoths and three wooly mammoths plus numerous other species. Their demise was caused by the sudden collapse of a sixty foot sinkhole.

The Devil's Tower, Black Hills of northeastern WY. 2000   Photo by Author

The Devil's Tower was included in the 1851 Sioux Nation Treaty. The Oglala Sioux call it Mato Tipila — interpreted as "Bear Lodge." The rock tower stands at 5,114 feet above sea level and was our first National Monument. The movie *CLOSE ENCOUNTERS OF THE THIRD KIND* was filmed here, but I do not think it mattered to Nellie. The "mash potato" scene was all that she cared to acknowledge. Something was disturbing her.

NELLIE'S CROSSING cont'd

Nellie at Devil's Tower, WY. July 10, 2000   Courtesy Altaffer Photography

SMELL of PINE

The smell of Ponderosa Pine was in the air as Nellie enjoyed dressing up for an old fashioned portrait in front of the great monolith rock called the Devil's Tower. "How did it get its name anyway?" Nellie asked.

The three of us viewed the rock tower from a lower circular trail at the bottom. Emory pushed and pushed as the wheelchair rounded the rock with Nellie in it. This rock tower rose 1,280 feet above the Belle Fourche River below.

That evening the fiery red sunset creating an eerie glow behind the tower was of no interest at all to this pious elderly woman. Alone, we walked out to capture a most magnificent sight.

The Devil's Tower under a blood red sky. 2000
Photographs by Author

Legend has it that seven little girls were chased by grizzlies to a low flat rock which carried them upward to keep them safe. The claws of the leaping bears left furrows on the sides of the ascending rock. The rock grew so high that the girls reached the sky and were transformed into the constellation known as the Pleiades (seven sisters).

In the morning we were off to Hell's Half Acre to get some repeat photography. The names Devil and Hell were most troubling to Nellie.

NELLIE'S CROSSING cont'd

Overlook near Buffalo, WY., Rt. 90. July 11, 2000   Photograph by Author

OVERWHELMED

Upon leaving the Devils Tower area, we were held up by a very long, slow freight train which fascinated Nellie far more than the giant monolith rock did.

Her chatter began nonstop. Nellie seemed jumpy and all over the keyboard. "Look at those snow capped mountains, I'll be darned — there wouldn't be many students out here — the grass seems to grow in clumps. You would need a lot of fans to keep cool," Nellie repeated over and over. Yes, it *was* exceptionally hot.

We camped at a Buffalo, WY. campground and prepared for our one day clockwise WY. "Loop Trip" to acquire repeat photography for *LAST CHANCE ALASKA*. We were searching for two of the RAD 1935 cross-country photos: *"Hell's Half Acre"* and *"Wind River Canyon."*

ONE DAY CLOCKWISE WY. LOOP TRIP

On July 12, 2000 we headed south on Route 25 to Casper, WY. The truck burned rubber as we pulled out of a gas station to arrive at Nellie's first *then and now* photo experience. Turning west onto Route 20/26 , we drove about 40 miles while Nellie took her fork, picked at her salad and enjoyed her Red Hots

Hell's Half Acre, WY. July 12, 2000   Photograph by Author

    The truck screeched to a stop as we noticed the Hell's Half Acre Motel sign. Nellie dropped her fork. We asked her if she would like to get out of the truck and stand under the motel sign for a picture, but adamantly Nellie didn't want anything to do with *that* sign. Yes, it was an *inferno* outside and Nellie was eighty-eight years old, so we had to respect her wishes, in spite of our disappointment. A 2001 "snow" shot was chosen instead. The movie STARSHIP TROOPERS used this site for the fictional planet of Klendatha. The land encompasses 960 acres. Other names given to this unusual area were: The Baby Grand Canyon, The Pits of Hades and The Devil's Kitchen.

NELLIE'S CROSSING cont'd

Hell's Half Acre, Rt. 20/26, WY. July 12, 2000 — Photograph by Author

CLOCKWISE WY. LOOP TRIP cont'd

Luck was with us, in spite of the area being closed. The owner was inside. He gave us permission to photograph on a small area of land extending out into the canyon. He was very much interested in the old 1935 photos of Hell's Half Acre, as he was a history teacher at the local high school and also a teacher of Political Science at a nearby college. He said the canyon was 550 foot deep. Years ago, there were red blinking eyes in one of the caves across the canyon for tourists to see.

In former days Indians drove great herds of buffalo into this depression for slaughter. Flint arrowheads and buffalo bones have been found here. A detachment of Bonneville's party visited this site in July 1833. This area has been dedicated to Natrona Co. by the Federal Government.

THEN and NOW

"Hell's Half Acre. May 12, 1935." RAD

Hell's Half Acre. July 12, 2001 JDH

Hell's Half Acre Motel, WY. July 12, 2000   Photographs by Author

In 2005 the motel/campground and restaurant closed for good. They have since been torn down. A return trip in 2001 was made for the repeat photo (lower left), which included a surprise snow fall.

Along the way to Shoshoni, WY. July 12, 2000

A sign reads "Shoshoni POP 497—ELEV. 4,820 ft," as our rig turns north to capture the *"Around the bend"* 1935 RAD shot.

NELLIE'S CROSSING cont'd

Photograph by Author
Nellie at Boysen State Park area, Rt 20 in WY. July 12, 2000

CLOCKWISE WY. LOOP TRIP cont'd

Wind River Canyon was the more difficult shot to achieve. Even Nellie was beginning to look. We eventually had to turn back and talk to someone at the Park Ranger Station at Boysen State Park. Heading north on Rt. 20/789 toward Thermopolis and Worland, we went through three tunnels in a row and there it was, the old photograph. It involved a drive by with the truck on a narrow, curvy road to achieve the *Then and Now* repeat image.

At Worland we turned east to Ten Sleep where we had dinner, followed by a unexpected awe-inspiring drive through Ten Sleep Canyon and on over the Powder River Pass to our campsite in Buffalo.

THEN and NOW

"Wind River Canyon, WY. ...looking N. May 14, 1935." RAD

Wind River Canyon, WY. July 12, 2000 JDH

Montana. border on Route 90. July 13, 2000   Photograph by Author

SEARCHING for the 1935 AUTO CAMP

We took Rt. 90 out of Buffalo, WY. and drove to the Montana border, continuing to look for the mysterious "*Auto camp area*" in the 1935 photo. Unsuccessful and tired of driving, we stopped at the Crazy Mountain Museum near Big Timber to ask some fruitless questions.

In 2001 we drove up to the Montana border on Rt. 120 south of Bridger and noticed the Cottonwood trees lining the Yellowstone River. This road was west of Rt. 90 and likely R.A.D.'s route of choice. The west entrance to Yellowstone is off this route and the pass was probably closed in 1935 due to snow. It was only mid-May.

THEN and NOW

"Auto camp in MT...dog 'Spot'... May 16, 1935." RAD   The Yellowstone River S. of Bridger, MT. 2001 JDH

NELLIE'S CROSSING cont'd

Photograph by Author
A 1912 Sourdough one room schoolhouse, Big Timber, MT. 2000

Courtesy of the museum next door, the school was opened for Nellie to go inside. One of the ladies was also born in 1912 which pleased both Nellie and the museum volunteer. Nellie could not wait to get into the schoolhouse. She ran up the steps to the school as if she was late for class. The photos taken of the 1912 school and museum area made for a successful stop.

In the distance to the north can be seen the Crazy Mountains. These mountains are home to several legends and the subject of a motion picture named *"Jeremiah Johnson."* The Indians called them mad mountains for their steepness and howling winds. The scenery from this area was also used in two other motion pictures, *"A River Ran Through It"* and *"The Horse Whisperer."*

THEN and NOW

"Crazy mountains, MT...snow covered...May 17, 1935" RAD

RT. 377 east of Big Timber, MT. 2001. JDH

Nellie in one room schoolhouse, Big Timber, MT. 2000   Photograph by Author

"JUST LIKE the SCHOOLHOUSE on the HILL," stated Nellie.

Inside the one room sourdough schoolhouse, Nellie took the seat she took so many years ago. *"There's George,"* she uttered before taking her seat. Playfully she said,*" Boys used to dip the girls pigtails in the ink wells."*

NELLIE'S CROSSING cont'd
THEN and NOW

"Lower falls of Yellowstone River — Grand Canyon of Yellowstone Park, WY... May 18, 1935"...RAD

Off to Yellowstone National Park on July 15, 2000, just like the prospectors of old, we entered by way of Gardiner and Rt. 89. Yellowstone National Park was established in 1872. It was our first National Park.

This exclusive photo (above) of the Lower Falls did not appear in *LAST CHANCE ALASKA,* but remained as part of the 1935 RAD Photo Collection until *NELLIE'S HILL.*

The Lower Falls, Yellowstone Nat'l Park, WY. July 15, 2000   Photo by JDH

Nellie's second one day loop trip was made — this time counter clockwise around Yellowstone National Park: Lower Geysers, Old Faithful and the "Grand Canyon" of Yellowstone, which included the Lower Falls. At these falls a repeat 1935 photograph was taken.

We didn't get back until midnight. Leaving the park, we regretted not taking a photograph of the moon over the entrance arch.

NELLIE'S CROSSING cont'd

THEN and NOW

The Lower Falls of Yellowstone National Park. 1994 JDH

Coincidentally, in 1994 the Lower Falls of Yellowstone National Park was reached by Snowmobile and a photograph was taken. At the time, we did not realize that six years later it would be visited for the purpose of repeat photography.

West Rt. 2 outside Butte, MT. 2000   Photograph by Author

In Butte we inquired about locating the Butte Pass for some repeat photography of a 1935 photograph. The gentlemen we had asked at a local coffee shop said that we were only fifteen minutes away.

Quote from *LAST CHANCE ALASKA*:

"Our home on wheels perched on a pass, posing for a photograph, while Nellie enjoyed views of the Continental Divide from inside the truck while munching a sandwich.

What an extraordinary journey it must have been chasing the cloud covered sun over the Bitterroot Range in Idaho on that gusty, gravel road back in nineteen thirty-five — with thoughts of Alaska becoming ever stronger in his head." JDH

THEN and NOW

"Crossing the Rockies near Butte, MT...3 inches snowfall the previous night ...May 19, 1935" RAD   West. Rt 2 outside Butte, MT. 2000 JDH

NELLIE'S CROSSING cont'd

Photograph by Author
WA.-ID border. Rt. 90. 2000

Wheat fields, dust devils and prairie as far as the eye could see met us after we crossed the Idaho border into Washington.

Photograph by UEH
Author and Nellie in front of the "newer" Vantage Bridge, WA. 2000

THEN and NOW

"Columbia River Canyon...near Vantage, WA. May 20, 1935" RAD

Columbia Gorge near Vantage, WA. 1999 JDH

Original old road entering the gorge. 2001   Photographs by Author

The original bridge over the Columbia River was built in 1927. Douglas traveled over it in 1935 on his way to Seattle. In 1968 the bridge was relocated by way of a barge down the Columbia River and up the Snake River to Lyon's Ferry State Park.

A dam was built to control flooding, help with irrigation and produce electricity for the area. The Columbia River stays at about forty-seven degrees year-round.

Relocated Vantage bridge, Lyon's Ferry State Park, WA. 2001

NELLIE'S CROSSING cont'd

Self-timer
Wanapum State Park overlooking the Basalt Cliffs, Vantage, WA. 2000

PICNIC in a COLUMBIA GORGE CAMPGROUND

The bigger picture was beginning to come into focus for Nellie. She was hearing more and more conversation about Alaska. Perhaps this was the picnic that needed to last forever.

Nellie's extraordinary cross-country road trip was coming to an end. Soon she would be spending some safe time by herself at the Weatherly Inn in Tacoma. An "Alaska Nellie" Douglas's wife would never be.

The family pet, "Little Jon" checked in at a very caring pet boarding facility named S.K.'s Pet Haven in Chehalis.

The job ahead was going to be a daunting endeavor. The seriousness of what we were attempting to do was upon us. Soon we would be picking up three of the four hikers at the SeaTac Airport in WA. and flying to Alaska. The plan was to backpack into the interior of Alaska to locate an old gold mining cabin and repeat photography taken in 1935-36. Pictures captured by Randolph Angus Douglas before he met and married Nellie.

In prepping for the hazardous hike into the interior we learned that the Ahtell Creek Valley was over-populated with grizzlies. The number six hundred was mentioned.

The Columbia River Gorge, Vantage, WA. 2000 Photograph by Author

This book is not in color, but words can't be written to describe how warm and glowing the sunset was over the gorge the night of our last campground picnic. It continued unyielding deep into the night until darkness finally came.

Late that evening, a most titanic, magnetic moon appeared, glimmering through the waters of the Columbia River Gorge. We were "sitting on the edge" and we knew it.

Words reiterated by the author over and over again were, *"I think I could swim across the Columbia Gorge,"* words brought on by months and months of swimming practice in a local gym to prepare for this trip.

I will speak only for myself, but a feeling of the *1935 prospector* (RAD) surrounding us was eerie and very real, but okay.

NELLIE'S CROSSING concluded

Photograph by Author
Nellie visits our Iron Creek campsite, WA. July 18, 2000

    Traveling over White Pass towards Randle, WA, Nellie proclaimed, *"Look to the right, Jill, and look at those Mountains. They are the highest I've ever seen."*

    Nellie was witnessing the breathtaking Mount Rainier in the distance and a section of the Cascade Range. Without doubt, a sight for her to behold. As our truck and camper turned left over the bridge in Randle, WA., we were met with a very well-kept campground. This campground was sitting close to Mount St. Helens National Park. The next day, we drove Nellie to the top and she could not get over all the dead wood laying around. She declared, *"Why did the city not get some prisoners to come up and clear all this wood off?"* But, that was an eighty-eight year old's take on the scene that stretched before her as far as the eye could see. No, an "Alaska Nellie" Douglas's wife would never be.

ALASKA

Trail to the Mineral Creek Glacier. Independence Mine, Hatcher Pass.
2000 UEH   2000 JDH

Iron Creek State Park was chosen by the hikers as the base camp for continuing all the way up to Alaska to attain repeat photography for *LAST CHANCE ALASKA*.

Photograph by Author
Hikers: Ulys Hopper, Ken and Alison Van Arsdel. Gold Cord Mine. 2000

BACK in the LOOP

Self-timer
Author, Nellie, Little Jon (dog) and Emory on Hurricane Ridge, WA. 2000

Nellie knew she was the hiker that was left behind and didn't mind letting us know about it. She sat there bravely in her wheelchair, after a fall, and smiled for a photo on Hurricane Ridge at the visitor center.

Port Angeles, WA. 2000 Photo by UEH

Jill and Nellie viewing inland waters of the Strait of Juan De Fuca looking south toward Port Angeles.

Recovery was quicker than expected and Nellie was soon out of her wheelchair and walking on her own.

Photo by JDH
Nellie and Emory (center) Port Angeles, WA. 2000

Olympic Peninsula, WA. 2000   Photo by JDH

CANADA

Speaking of leaves, Nellie does turn Canadian for just ONE day. The three of us (including Little Jon) ferry up to Victoria, Canada to visit Butchart Gardens, B.C.

OBSTRUCTION POINT, WA.

Nellie (below R) insisted on carrying a pack for a short hike on the Obstruction Point Trail. The trail from Obstruction Point to Deer Park is 7.4 miles and is stated as Moderate by the National Park Service in WA. It's unique feature is that it is the highest trail in the Olympic National Park. The elevation change is from 6,100 feet to 5,400 feet. Later, Nellie does not see her daughter walking the "Goat Trail" around the corner, while she catches her breath in the truck.

L Photo by UEH and R Photo by JDH

Jill (above L) is in a reckless mood, as her birthday is just days away. A 1,000 foot roll down the sand stone with nothing to hang on to awaits a "slip." 2000

BACK in the LOOP cont'd

Nellie at Neah Bay, WA. Sept., 2000   Photographs by Author

Before leaving for home, the three of us drove the west coast of the Olympic Peninsula and walked through the Hoe Rain Forest.

Nellie inside the camper at Conestoga Quarters, WA. Sept., 2000

Decaf? Negative. Nellie always liked her morning coffee strong. A lift just before leaving...and then it was time to hit the road.

CHAPTER VI
EASTWARD HO

Emory and Nellie. Olympic Peninsula, WA. 2000   Photograph by Author

At our Campground near Port Angeles, WA., Emory makes repairs as we prepare for the long road trip back to Florida.

EASTWARD HO

Photograph by UEH
Heading east. Oregon Trail Museum in Flagstaff Hill, OR. Oct. 1, 2000

Remnants and markers from the Oregon Trail were everywhere. On the beginning of our journey east, we took a side trip to the National Historic Oregon Trail Center in Flagstaff Hill Oregon.

The Center reminded us that travel trailers and motor homes are the covered wagons of today. Below is our truck and travel trailer heading west in S. D. in 2000, exemplifying the comparison.

South Dakota. July 7, 2000   Photograph by Author

Nellie on drive to Redcliff, CO. Oct. 5, 2000

After a day of exploring in Vail, Colorado, we took a side trip to Radcliff. We saw attention-grabbing snow in the tall fir trees along the way and on the distant mountains, making for an enjoyable drive.

> *"Did I ever tell you, you are a real trooper?" said the Author to Nellie, while the truck droned on. "No," spoke Nellie. Jill repeated, "You are a real trooper" "Thank you," said Nellie.*

Getting stuck in a snow bank while parking to take some alluring photos, discouraged us from traveling further on the desolate road we were on. We never made it all the way to Radcliff.

Photographs by Author

EASTWARD HO cont'd

Photograph by Author

THE WORLD ACCORDING to NELLIE

LETTER 42
REGARDING ILLEGAL DRUG USE

I never heard about anyone using hard drugs. I do not believe in making anything legal that is harmful to our youth.   N.C.D

LETTER 43
REGARDING TOBACCO

Smoking was not allowed in my early school years. However, I do remember that some of the eighth graders would fool around behind the school and smoke.   N.C.D.

LETTER 44   *ERA of PROHIBITION*

If the older people wanted alcohol, they got it. Controlling a lot of things like that is not too successful in the long run. People who want it will always find a way to get it. Those that don't use stuff like alcohol etc. will leave it alone. Each person has to decide how he wants to live.   N.C.D.

ALMOST NINE DECADES

Oh my, people of almost nine decades do have an opinion. Theirs was the most progressive century of all time. It started so "horse and buggy" and ended up so "digital."

When computers were as large as a wall, her husband, Randolph, had told his young grandson, Ken, that they were just a fad. An interesting deduction, but one that proved completely wrong. Ken is now working in Silicon Valley.

Vail, Colorado, elevation 10,662 Ft. October 5, 2000 Photograph by Author

Golden leaves were everywhere.

Breathing, nausea and headache were a problem for a while for me. We all drank plenty of water — Nellie did not seem to be bothered by the altitude, though. Perhaps she was in her element, as skiing was part of her childhood upbringing.

The only thing that bothered Emory in Vail were the high diesel prices. He filled up the tank saying, "ouch," at the $2.00 a gallon sign.

Before leaving Colorado, it had begun to snow.

103

EASTWARD HO cont'd

The Texas border. Sunday, October 8, 2000   Photograph by Author

It had been discussed on the drive back that we will have to be making a second trip up to the mainland of Alaska to complete the repeat photography for *LAST CHANCE ALASKA*. While returning to Florida, a visit was made in Texas to Nellie's son, Daniel and his family where arrangements for Nellie's final direction change were discussed.

Instead of flying to Alaska, this time we will drive. We will camp through British Columbia and the Yukon Territory, taking the most northerly route through Dawson City (home of the Klondike Gold Rush of August, 1896). Once in Alaska, three and a half months will be spent interviewing locals and following up on necessary repeat photography.

Little Jon (dog) on a Texas oil rig. 2000   Photograph by Author

Under dim light, maps of British Columbia and the Yukon Territory were opened and spread out. The 1935 *"Auto Camp"* photo was still not located, nor was the 1935 *"Crazy Mountains"* photo. All the unallocated lower forty-eight sights will be searched for on our 2001 cross-country journey to the Washington -Canadian border.

Nellie was an integral part of three of the repeat photos in 2000: The 1935 *"Wind River Canyon"* photo in Wyoming and the 1935 *"Butte Pass"* photo in Montana for *Last Chance Alaska* and the 1935 *"Lower Falls"* photo in Yellow Stone National Park for *"Nellie's Hill."*

We will miss her on our second leg of this trip, but it will be an arduous excursion and no place for an eighty-nine year old woman.

After crossing the border in Washington, we plan to travel up through British Columbia, going through Prince George, Chetwynd and Fort Nelson up to the Yukon border.

In the Yukon Territory, we will stop or pass through Watson Lake, Whitehorse, Carmacks, Pelly Crossing, Dawson City and on to the Top of the World Highway arriving at the Yukon-Alaska border crossing.

In Alaska we will pass through Chicken, Tok, Slana, Chistochina, Gakona, Glennallen and on to our base camp in Valdez.

EASTWARD HO concluded

Nellie at the Florida line. 2000   Photograph by Author

NELLIE'S TRIP THOUGHTS

"*One thing I learned is that our military is strong and that we could tighten up in a hurry.*

I feel it was a very successful trip. It was a long trip — we have a very big country. I put it number one in my book."

CHAPTER VII
A PRECIOUS FEW

Together again, Nellie and Ruby (cat). 2000

It was the evening of October, Friday the thirteenth when we arrived back from the west coast. After many long days of driving, Nellie couldn't wait to see her Ruby. After all, we had been away over three and a half months. Ruby arrived back on Saturday. Nellie's grandson, Ken drove Ruby over from Orlando and they were together again.

In spite of our arrival date, the trip was anything but unlucky. Nothing was lost or stolen along the way. There weren't any accidents on the road and the house looked fine. Nellie was in good spirits and healthier and spunkier than ever, in spite of a few mishaps along the way. It was an incredible journey for a woman just a year and a half away from celebrating ninety. Her final quote was, "I don't think we should have to cross the country too often."

Sunday, I realized Nellie's days here in Florida were coming to an end. We vowed to do something fun every Sunday until we left.

A PRECIOUS FEW cont'd

Self-timer

Nellie, Little Jon (dog), Emory and the Author, Jill
Tomoka State Park. 2000

Sundays breezed along in the Florida sun. Tomoka State Park, Spook Hill and the Bok Singing Tower in Lake Whales were all visited. We celebrated holidays as they rolled along knowing all too well that time was running out and the countdown to leaving would soon be upon us.

Time was also running out for our little family pet, Little Jon. He passed away suddenly on February 9, 2001 from heart issues and never made it to Alaska as we had hoped.

The last week hit suddenly, not only was Nellie saying goodbye to Florida, but she was saying goodbye to her much-loved Ruby.

Nellie will be having her big ninetieth birthday party in Texas, after we return from Alaska.

DAY SIX. April 4, 2001

The countdown to leaving began and Nellie wrote:

> *"I am going to miss the view from the front porch. There is always activity going on. I like hearing the trains and hearing the birds sing."*

DAY SIX of the COUNT-DOWN cont'd

Sitting on a porch chair in the warm morning Florida breezes, Nellie Continues...

"The Jasmine smells so sweet and the lilies at the corner of the house are in full bloom. They are gorgeous."

Then she remembered, Jill said, *" It will be time to leave when the lilies bloom."*

Lilies at the corner. FL., 2001   Photos by Author

Nellie's last Florida birthday celebration was in March, 2001, just before we all headed west *"once again."* Days five, four, three, two and one went by quickly as the Odyssey blasted off for Mars, the Space Coast received its new "321" area code.

Nellie lived with us nearly four years. She was eighty-six years old when she arrived in Florida.

HAPPY "eighty-ninth" BIRTHDAY
Nellie Clarke Douglas

A PRECIOUS FEW

FLORIDA DEPARTURE

The "for sale" sign went up, though not understood. Nellie sat in her chair and watched as our boxes were all packed and dishes wrapped. There wasn't time for laughter, nor time for games — minutes marched on in this quiet, empty place. Nellie had been through moves before, but this one seemed different.

"To stay in this house forever" was spoken again and again. Reality took an awful turn, as we said farewell to "224" that morning. This time, when the fall leaves came they came to stay.

If she had her way she would have gone back to her New Jersey home and continued teaching her music, *or* would she have preferred "the hill?" I think I know where she really wanted to be.

TEXAS

A Texas birthday celebration. 2002   Photograph by Author

Remembering Babe? 2002   Photograph by Author

Growing up in our northern New Jersey home, there was always a black "mama" cat around. Through the years cat sagas flourished. Ruby did make a surprise visit to Nellie in her Texas residence one Christmas.

Photographer unknown
Nellie and Babe on the "hill." N.Y. State, circa early 1920's

Nellie, eighty-nine years old. 2001   Photograph by Author

There are a lot of *Nellie's* in this world, but only one who lived on a hill overlooking the Utica valley in upstate New York during the very early 1900's.

"When an old person dies, it is like a library burning down." unknown

Made in the USA
Charleston, SC
10 April 2015